*Nature Spirits
and Elementals*

By
Louise Off

Copyright © 2022 Lamp of Trismegistus. All rights reserved. No part of this publication may be reproduced or transmitted in any form or by any means, electronic or mechanical, including photocopying, recording, or by any information storage and retrieval system, without permission in writing from Lamp of Trismegistus. Reviewers may quote brief passages.

ISBN: 978-1-63118-605-9

Esoteric Classics

Other Books in this Series and Related Titles

Aurora of the Philosophers by Paracelsus (978-1-63118-507-6)

Rosicrucian Rules, Secret Signs, Codes and Symbols by various (978-1-63118-488-8)

On the Philadelphian Gold by Philochrysus & Philadelphus (978-1-63118-511-3)

Paracelsus, the Four Elements and Their Spirits by M P Hall (978-1-63118-400-0)

The Stone of the Philosophers by A E Waite (978-1-63118-509-0)

Clairvoyance and Psychic Abilities by A Besant &c (978-1-63118-403-1)

The Rosicrucian Chemical Marriage by Christian Rosenkreuz (978-1-63118-458-1)

The Alchemical Catechism of Paracelsus by Paracelsus (978-1-63118-513-7)

Alchemy in the Nineteenth Century by Helena P. Blavatsky (978-1-63118-446-8)

Rosicrucians and Speculative Masonry in the Seventeenth Century (978-1-63118-489-5)

Qabbalistic Teachings and the Tree of Life by M P Hall (978-1-63118-482-6)

The Sepher Yetzirah and the Qabalah by M P Hall (978-1-63118-481-9)

The Devil in Love by Jacques Cazotte (978–1–63118–499–4)

Fortune-Telling with Dice by Astra Cielo (978-1-63118-466-6)

History, Analysis and Secret Tradition of the Tarot by Hall &c (978-1-63118-445-1)

Crystal Vision Through Crystal Gazing by Frater Achad (978-1-63118-455-0)

The Golden Verses of Pythagoras: Five Translations (978-1-63118-479-6)

Arcane Formulas or Mental Alchemy by W W Atkinson (978-1-63118-459-8)

The Machinery of the Mind by Dion Fortune (978-1-63118-451-2)

The A E Waite Reader: A Selection of Occult Essays (978-1-63118-515-1)

The Leadbeater Reader: A Selection of Occult Essays (978-1-63118-483-3)

Audio versions are also available on Audible, Amazon and Apple

Other Books in this Series and Related Titles

Swedenborg Bifrons by H P Blavatsky (978-1-63118-604-2)

Practical Use of Psychic Powers by C W Leadbeater (978-1-63118-603-5)

Using White & Black Magic by C W Leadbeater (978-1-63118-602-8)

Jesus, the Last Great Initiate by Edouard Schure (978-1-63118-599-1)

Mysterious Wonders of Antiquity by Manly P Hall (978-1-63118-598-4)

Ancient Mysteries and Secret Societies by Manly P Hall (978–1–63118–597–7)

The Zodiac and Its Signs by Manly P Hall (978–1–63118–596–0)

Life and Teachings of Hermes Trismegistus by Manly P Hall (978–1–63118–595–3)

The Secrets of Doctor Taverner by Dion Fortune (978–1–63118–594–6)

Vegetarianism, Theosophy & Occultism by Leadbeater &c (978–1–63118–593–9)

Applied Theosophy by Henry S Olcott (978–1–63118–592–2)

Higher Consciousness by C W Leadbeater (978–1–63118–591–5)

Theories About Reincarnation and Spirits by H P Blavatsky (978–1–63118–590–8)

The Use and Power of Thought by C W Leadbeater (978–1–63118–589–2)

Commentary on the Pymander by G R S Mead (978–1–63118–588–5)

Hypnotism and Mesmerism by Annie Besant (978–1–63118–587–8)

Spirits of Various Kinds by Helena P Blavatsky (978–1–63118–586–1)

The Hidden Language of Symbolism by Annie Besant (978–1–63118–585–4)

Eastern Magic & Western Spiritualism by Henry S Olcott (978–1–63118–584–7)

Spiritual Progress and Practical Occultism by H P Blavatsky (978–1–63118–583–0)

Memory and Consciousness by Besant & Blavatsky (978–1–63118–582–3)

Audio versions are also available on Audible, Amazon and Apple

Table of Contents

Introduction...7

Nature-Spirits or Elementals...9

The Difference Between Elementals and Elementaries...29

INTRODUCTION

The word "esoteric" can be difficult to define. Esotericism in general can be seen less as a system of beliefs and more as a category, which encompasses numerous, different systems of beliefs. It's a bit of juxtaposition, since the word "esoteric" indicates something that few people know about, while the term itself broadly covers numerous philosophies, practices, areas of study and belief systems.

In a greater sense, Esotericism acts as a storehouse for secret knowledge, which is often considered ancient (by *tradition, if not by fact*), passed down from generation to generation, in private. At various times in history, simply possessing the knowledge of some of these subjects, was considered illegal and a jailable offence, if discovered. This usually included such general topics as Alchemy, Pharmacology, Qabalah, Hermeticism, Occultism, Ceremonial Magic, Astrology, Divination, Rosicrucianism and so on. Collectively, these areas of study were often referred to as the esoteric sciences.

Sometimes, the outer garment of a subject isn't esoteric, while what is hidden beneath it, is. As an example, Freemasonry isn't necessarily esoteric by nature (at *least not anymore*), but certain signs, passwords and handshakes given to the candidate during their initiation, are in fact, esoteric, in the sense that they are hidden from the general public.

Today, in the twenty-first century, such topics are readily available at bookstores across the country, and numerous main-steam publishers offer beginners guides and coffee-table volumes on many of these subjects, intended for mass appeal. Books like *"The Secret"* have turned previously arcane topics into household knowledge. All that being the case, however, it isn't to say that there still aren't buried secrets to uncover, ancient wisdom being ignored and forgotten mysteries to be explored. In fact, it is often that we are only able to further our own studies by standing on the shoulders of these disappearing giants.

Lamp of Trismegistus is doing its part to help preserve humanity's esoteric history by making some of these classics available to those students who are seeking to unearth the knowledge of these ancient colossi.

So, be sure to check other titles from our *Esoteric Classics* series, as well as our *Occult Fiction, Theosophical Classics, Foundations of Freemasonry Series, Supernatural Fiction, Paranormal Research Series, Studies in Buddhism* and our *Christian Apocrypha Series*. You can also download the audio versions of most of these titles from Amazon, Apple or Audible, for learning on the go.

NATURE-SPIRITS OR ELEMENTALS

"Life is one all-pervading principle, and even the thing that seems to die and putrify but engenders new life and changes to new forms of matter. Reasoning, then, by analogy — il not a leaf, if not a drop of water, but is, no less than yonder star, a habitable and breathing world, common sense would suffice to teach that the circumfluent Infinite, which you call space — the boundless Impalpable which divides the earth from the moon and stars — is filled also with its correspondent and appropriate life." — ZANONI.

Within the last fifty years the human mind has been awakening slowly to the fact that there is a world, invisible to ordinary powers of vision, existing in close juxtaposition to the world cognised by our material senses. This world, or condition of existence for more etherial beings, has been variously called — Spirit-world, Summer-land, Astral-world, Hades, Kama-loca, or Desire-world, etc. Slowly and with difficulty do ideas upon the nature and characteristics of this world dawn upon the modern mind. The imagination, swayed by pictures of sensuous life, revels in the fantastic imagery it attributes to this unknown and dimly conceived state of existence, more often picturing what is false than what is true. Generally speaking, the most crude conceptions are entertained; these embrace but two conditions of life, the embodied and disembodied, for which there are only the earth and heaven, or hell, with that intermediate state accepted by Roman Catholics, called Purgatory. There is, therefore, for such minds, only two orders of beings, *i.e.*, mankind, and angels or devils, categorically termed "spirits"; but what would be the mode of life of those "spirits", is a subject upon which ordinary intellects can throw no light at all. Their ideas are walled in by an impenetrable darkness, and not a ray of light glimmers across the unfathomable gulf lying beyond the grave; that portal of death which, for them, opens upon unknown darkness, and closes upon the light, vivacity, and gaiety of the earth.

The idea that the beings we would term *disembodied* do actually inhabit bodies of an aerial substance, invisible to our grosser senses, in a world exactly suited to their needs, surpasses the comprehension of an ordinary understanding, which can conceive only of gross matter, visible and tangible. Yet science begins to talk of *mind-stuff*, or *soul-substance*, in reality that etherial substance which ranks next to dense matter, and which it wears as an external, more hardened shell. For there is space within space. Once realising the existence of an *inner world*, we shall find that all our ideas concerning space, time, and every particular of our existence, and the world we live in must become entirely revolutionised.

The principal source of knowledge which has been opened in modern times concerning the next state of existence has revealed itself in a manner homogeneous to itself. It has come by an interior method — a revelation from within acting upon the without. The inner world, although always acting upon and through its external covering, in a hidden or veiled way, as from an inscrutable cause, has manifested itself in a manner more overt and cognisable by the bodily senses of man. At least that which has usually been termed, with more or less awe, the "supernatural", the "ghostly", has impinged upon the mental incrassation of sensual man as a thing to be reckoned with in daily life; no longer to be relegated to the region of vague darkness *d'outre tombe*. Hence the human mind is being awakened to study and dive into the depths of that life within life, wherein dwell the disembodied, the so-called *dead*, the angels, and, *per contra*, the devils. Those hidden aerial and etherial regions, wherein the *souls* of things, and beings, draw life from the bosom of Nature: wherein they find their *active* habitat: wherein Nature keeps a store of objects more wonderful, and infinitely more varied, than serve for her regions of dense matter: wherein man can discern the occult causes and beginnings of all things, even of his own thoughts; and whereupon he learns, at length, that he possesses the power of projecting by thought-creation forms more or less endued with life and intelligence, which compose his mental world, and with which he, as it were, "peoples space". He finds the sphere of his responsibilities immensely enlarged by this new knowledge, of which he is taking the first honeyed sips, delighted with the self-importance which the heretofore unsuspected power of diving into the unseen seems to bestow. If hitherto he has had to hold himself responsible for the consequences of his external actions, that they should not militate against the order of society as regards the laws of morality and virtue, he has at least acted upon the impression that his *secret thoughts* were his own, and remained with him, affecting no one but himself; were incognisable in their veiled chambers, and of which it was not necessary to take any notice: the transitory, evanescent, spontaneous workings of mind, unknown, and inscrutable, which begin and end like the flight of a bird, whence coming and where going it is impossible to know.

By the first faint gleams of the light of hidden wisdom, which are beginning to dawn upon his mind, he now perceives that responsibility does not end upon the plane of earth, but extends into the aerial regions of that inner world where his thoughts are no longer secret, and where they affect the astral currents, acting for the good or detriment of others to almost infinite extent, That he may act upon the ambient atmospheres, not only of the outer but inner planes of life, like a plant of poisonous exhalations, if his thoughts be not pure and good; peopling *unseen* space with the outcome of a debased mind, in the shape of hideous and maleficent creatures. He becomes responsible, therefore, for the consequences of his mental actions and thought-life, as well as those actions carefully prepared to pass unchallenged before this world's gaze.

Diving into the unseen by the light of the new spiritual knowledge now radiating into all minds, we learn that there are three degrees of life in man, the material, the aerial, and the etherial, corresponding to body, soul, and spirit; and that there are three corresponding planes of existence inhabited by beings suited to them.

The subject of our paper will limit us at present to the aerial, or soul-plane — the next contiguous, or astral world. The beings that more especially live in this realm of the soul, have by common consent been termed "Elementals". Nature in illimitable space teems with life in forms etherial, evanescent as thought itself, or more objectively condensed and solidified, according to the inherent attraction which holds them together; enduring according to the force, energy, or power which gave them birth; intelligent, or non-intelligent, from the same source, which is mental. These spirits of the soul-world are possessed of aerial bodies, and their world has its own firmament, its own atmosphere and conditions of existence, its own objects, scenes, habitations. Yet their world and the world of man intermingle, interpenetrate, and "throw their shadows upon each other", says Paracelsus. Again, he says: "As there is in our world water and fire, harmonies and contrasts, visible bodies and invisible essences, likewise these beings are varied in their constitution, and have their own peculiarities, for which human beings have no comprehension".

Matter, as known to men in bodies, is seen and felt by means of the physical senses; but to beings not provided with such senses, the things of our world are as invisible and intangible as things of more etherial substance are to our grosser senses. Elementals which find their habitat in the interior of the earth's shell, usually called "*gnomes*" are not conscious of the density of the element of earth as we perceive it; but breathe in a free atmosphere, and behold objects of which we cannot form the remotest conception. In like manner exist the *Undines* in water, *Sylphs* in air, and *Salamanders* in fire". The Elementals of the Air, Sylphs, are said to be friendly towards man; those of the water, Undines, are malicious. The Salamanders can, but rarely do, associate with man, "on account of the fiery nature of the element they inhabit". The Pigmies (gnomes) are friendly; but as they are the guardians of treasure they usually oppose the approach of man, baffling by many mysterious arts the selfish greed of seekers for buried wealth. We, however, read of their alluring miners either by stroke of pick, or hammer, or by floating lights to the best mineral " leads." Paracelsus says of these subterranean elementals that they build houses, vaults, and strange-looking edifices of certain immaterial substances unknown to us. " They have some kind of alabaster, marble, cement, etc., but these substances are as different from ours as the web of a spider is different from our linen".

These inhabitants of the elements, or "nature-spirits", may, or may not be, conscious of the existence of man; oftentimes feeling him merely as a force which propels, or arrests them; for by his will and by his thought, he acts upon the astral currents of the aerial world in which they live; and. by the use of his hands he sways the material elements of earth, fire, and water wherein they are established. They perceive the soul-essence of man with its "currents and forms", and they also are capable of reading such thoughts as do not spiritually transcend their powers of discernment. They perceive the states of feeling and emotions of men by the "*colours* and impressions produced in their auras", and may thus irresistibly be drawn into overt action upon man's plane of life. They are the invisible *stone-throwers* we hear of so frequently, supposed to be *human* spirits; the perpetrators of mischief, such as destruction of property in the habitations of men, noises, and mysterious nocturnal annoyances.

Of all writers upon occult subjects to whose works we have as yet gained access, Paracelsus throws the greatest light upon these tricky sprites celebrated in the realm of poesy, and inhabiting that disputed land popularly termed Fairydom. From open vision, and that wonderful insight of the "master" or adept into the secrets of nature, Paracelsus is able to give us the most positive information concerning their bodily formation, the nature of their existence, and other extraordinary particulars, which prove that he has actually seen and observed them, and doubtless also *employed* them as the obedient servants of his purified will: a power into which the *spiritual man* ascends by a species of right, when he has thrown off, or conquered, the thraldom of matter in his own body, and stands open-eyed at "the portals of his deep within".

We will quote certain extracts from the pages of this wonderful interpreter of Nature. "There are two kinds of flesh. One that comes from Adam, and another that does not come from Adam. The former is gross material, visible and tangible for us; the other one is not tangible and not made from earth. If a man who is a descendant from Adam wants to pass through a wall, he will have first to make a hole through it; but a being who is not descended from Adam needs no hole nor door, but may pass through matter that appears solid to us without causing any damage to it. The beings not descended from Adam, as well as those descended from him, are organised and have substantial bodies; but there is as much difference between the substance composing their bodies as there is between Matter and Spirit. Yet the Elementals are not Spirits, because they have flesh, blood, and bones; they live and propagate offspring; they eat and talk, act and sleep, etc., and consequently they cannot be properly called 'spirits'. They are beings occupying a place between man and spirits, resembling men and women in their organization and form, and resembling spirits in the rapidity of their locomotion. They are intermediary beings or Composita, formed out of two parts joined into one; just as two colours mixed together will appear as one colour, resembling neither one nor the other of the two original ones. The Elementals have no higher principles; they are therefore not immortal, and when they die they perish like animals. Neither water nor fire can injure them, and they cannot be locked up in our material prisons. They are, however, subject to diseases. Their costumes, actions, forms, ways of speaking, etc., are not very unlike those of human beings; but there are a great many varieties. They have only animal intellects, and are incapable of spiritual development".

In saying the Elementals have "no higher principles", and "When they die they perish like animals", Paracelsus does not stop to explain that the higher principles in them are absolutely latent, as in plants; and that animals in "perishing" are not destroyed, but the psychical or soul-part of the animal passes, by the processes of evolution, into higher forms.

"Each species moves only in the element to which it belongs, and neither of them can go out of its appropriate element, which is to them as the air is to us, or the water to fishes; and none of them can live in the element belonging to another class. To each elemental being the element in which it lives is transparent, invisible, and respirable, as the atmosphere is to ourselves". "As far as the personalities of the Elementals are concerned, it may be said that those belonging to the element of water resemble human beings of either sex; those of the air are greater and stronger; the Salamanders are long, lean, and dry; the Pigmies (Gnomes) are the length of about two spans, but they may extend or elongate their forms until they appear like giants".

"Nymphs (undines, or naiads) have their residences and palaces in the element of water; Sylphs and Salamanders have no fixed dwellings. Salamanders have been seen in the shape of fiery balls, or tongues of fire running over the fields or appearing in houses", or at physical séances as starry lights, darting and dancing about.

"There are certain localities where large numbers of Elementals live together, and it has occurred that a man has been admitted into their communities and lived with them for a while, and that they have become visible and tangible to him".

Poets, in their moments of exaltation, have an unconscious soul-vision before which Nature's invisible worlds lie like an open volume, and they translate her secrets into language of mystic meanings whose harmonies are re-interpreted by sympathetic minds. The poet Hogg, in his "*Rapture of Kilmeny*", would seem to have had a vision of some such visit as that described above, into the fairyland of pure, peaceful *Elementals*.

"Bonny Kilmeny gaed up the glen" — and is represented as having fallen asleep. During this sleep she is transported to " a far countrye," whose gentle, lovely inhabitants receive her with delight. The following lines reveal the poet's power of inner vision, as will be seen by the words italicised. They are in wonderful accord with the descriptions given by Paracelsus from the actual observation of a *conscious seer*. —

"They lifted Kilmeny, they led her away,
And she walk'd *in the light of a sunless day*;
The sky was *a dome of crystal bright*,
The *fountain of vision and fountain of light*;
The emerald fields *were of dazzling glow*,
And the *flowers of everlasting blow*."

It needs but a brushing away of the films of flesh, which occurs in moments of rapt inspiration, for the soul, escaping from its prison-house, to revel in the innocent, peaceful scenes of its own inner world, and give a true description of what it beholds. The inner meanings of things, the symbolical correspondences are revealed in a flash of light, and the poet-soul becomes revelator and prophet all in one. He sets it down to imagination and fancy, when he returns into his normal state, and it is what we call "a flight of genius", —

the power of the soul to enter its own appropriate world. Certainly "*les âmes de boue*" have no such power. It is, however, a *proof that world exists*, if we will but understand it aright.

There has never existed a poet with a truer conception of "elemental life" than Shakspeare. What more exquisite creation of the poet's fancy, which *might be every word of it true*, for in no particular does it surpass the truth, than that of *Ariel*, whom the "foul witch Sycorax", "by help of her more potent ministers, and in her most unmitigable rage", did confine "into a cloven pine"; for Ariel, the good "elemental", was "a spirit too delicate to act her earthly and abhorred commands". When Prospero, the Adept and White Magician, arrived upon the scene, by his superior art he liberated the delicate Ariel, who afterwards becomes his ministering servant for *good*, not for evil.

In the "Midsummer Night's Dream" Titania transports a human child into her elemental world, where she keeps him with so jealous a love as to refuse to yield him even to her "fairy lord", as Puck calls him. Puck himself is almost as exquisite a realisation of "elemental" life as Ariel. As Shakespeare unfolds the lovely, innocent tale of the occupations, sports and pranks of this aerial people, he introduces us to the elementals of his own beautiful thought world; and, although indulging in the "sports of fancy"; there is so broad a foundation of truth, that, being enlightened by the revelations of Paracelsus, we no longer think we are merely entertained by the poetical inventions of a master of his art, but may well believe we have been witnesses of a charming reality beheld through the "rift in the veil" of the poet's unconscious inner sight. Indeed, one of the tenets of occult science is that there is nothing on earth, nor that the mind of man can conceive, which is not already existent in the unseen world.

We reflect in the translucence, or "*diaphane*" of our mental world those concrete images of things which we attract by the irresistible magnetism of *desire* working through the thought. It is a spontaneous, unconscious mental process with us; but there is no reason why it should not become a perfectly conscious process regulated by a divine wisdom to functions of harmony with nature's laws, and to productions of beauty and beneficence for the good of the whole world. As the world is the concreted emanation of Divine Thought, so it is by thought that man, the microcosm, *creates* upon his petty, finite plane. Given the desire — even if it be only as the lightest breath of a summer zephyr upon the sleeping bosom of the ocean, scarcely ruffling its surface — it becomes a centre of attraction for suitable molecules of thought-substance floating in space, which immediately "agglomerate round the idea proceeding to reveal itself", *bymeans* of clothing itself in substance. By these silent processes in the invisible world wherein our souls draw the breath of life, we form our mental world, our personal character, even our very physical bodies. The *perisprit*, or astral body, the vehicle for *formless spirit*, is essentially built up from the mental life, and grows by the accretion of those atoms or molecules of thought-substance which are assimilable by the mind. Hence a good man a man of lofty aspirations, forms, as the *nearest* external clothing of his inner spirit, a beautiful soul-body, which irradiates through and beautifies the physical body. The man of low and grovelling mind will, on the contrary, attract the depraved and poisoned substances of the lower astral world; the malarial emanations thrown off by other equally depraved beings, by which his mind becomes embruted, his soul diseased, whilst his physical form presents in a concrete image the ugliness of his inner nature. Such a man never ascends above the dense, mephitic vapours of the sin-laden world, nor takes into his soul the slightest breath of pure, vitalising air. He is diseased by invisible astral *microbes*, being most effectually self-inoculated with them by the operation of desires which never transcend the earth. Did we lift the veil which shrouds from mortal sight the elemental world of such a moral pervert, we should behold a world teeming with hideous forms, and as actively working as the *bacteria* of fermentation revealed by a powerful microscope, elementals of destruction, death, and decay, which must pass out into other forms for the purification of the spiritual atmosphere; creatures produced by the man's own thoughts, living upon and in him, and reflecting, like mirrors, his hideousness back again to himself. It is from the presence of innumerable foci of evil of this kind that the world is befouled, and the moral atmosphere of our planet tainted.' They emit poisoned astral currents, from which none are safe but those who are in the *positive* condition of perfect moral health.

From the Fountain of Life we draw in the materials of life, and become, upon our lower plane, other living fountains, which from liberty of choice, and freedom of will, have the power of so muddying the pure stream, that in its turbidness and foulness it becomes death instead of life, and produces hell instead of heaven. When we, by self-purification, and that constant mental discipline which trains us upwards, clinging to our highest ideal by the tendrils of faith, and love, and continual aspiration, as the vine would cling to a rock — have eliminated all that is impure in our thought world, we become fountains of life, and make our own heavens, wherein are reflected only images of divine beauty. The whole elemental world on our immediate astral plane becomes gradually transformed during the progress of our evolution into the higher spiritual grades of being. And as humanity *en masse* advances, throwing off the moral and spiritual deformity of the selfish, ignorant Ego, the astral atmospheres belonging to our planet world become filled with "elementals" of a peaceful, loving character, of beautiful forms, and of beneficent influences. The currents of evil force which now act with a continually jarring effect upon those striving to maintain the equilibrium of harmony with Nature upon the side of *good*, would cease. That depression, agitation, and distress which now, from inscrutable causes, assail minds otherwise rejoicing in an innocent happiness, forewarning them of some impending calamity, or of some evil presence it seems impossible to shake off, would become unknown. The horrible demons of War, with which humanity, in its sinful state of *separateness*, is continually threatening itself, — as if the members of one body were self-opposed, and revolting from that state of agreement that can alone ensure the well-being of the whole — would no longer be held, like ravenous bloodhounds chafing against their leashes, ready to spring, at a word, upon their hellish work; but they will have passed away, like other hideous deformities of evil; and the serene astral atmospheres would no longer reflect ideas of cruel wrongs to fellow-beings, revenge, lust of power, injustice, and ruthless hatred. We are taught that around an "idea" agglomerate the suitable molecules of soul-substance — "Monads" as Leibnitz terms them, until a concrete form stands created, the production of a mind, or minds. All the hideous man-created beings, powers or forces, which now act like ravaging pestilences and storms in the astral atmospheres of our planet will have disappeared like the monstrous phantoms of a frightful dream, when the whole of humanity has progressed into a state of higher spiritual evolution. It is well to reflect that *each individual*, however humble and apparently insignificant his position in the great human family, can aid by his life, by the silent emanation of his pure and wise thoughts, as well as by his active labours for humanity, in bringing nearer this halcyon period of peace, harmony, and purity — that millennium, in short, we are all looking forward to, as a dream we can never hope to see realised.

In " *Man:_Fragments_of Forgotten_History*," we read: "Violence was the most baneful manifestation of man's spiritual decadence, and it rebounded upon him from the elemental beings, whom it was his duty to develop"— those *sub-mundanes*, towards whom man is now learning he incurs *responsibilities* of which he is at present utterly unconscious, but of which he will indubitably become more and more aware as he ascends the ladder of spiritual evolution.

To continue our extract from "*Fragments*": "When this duty was ignored, and the separation of interests was accentuated, the natural man forcibly realised an antagonism with the elemental spirits. As violence increased in man, these spirits waxed strong in their way, and, true to their natures, which had been outraged by the neglect of those who were in a sense their guardians, they automatically responded with resentment. No longer could man rely upon the power of love or harmony to guide others, because he himself had ceased to be impelled solely by its influence; distrust had marred the symmetry of his inner self, and beings who could not perceive but only *receive impressions projected towards them*, quickly adapted themselves to the altered conditions". — (Elementals as "forces", respond to forces, or are swayed by them; man, as a superior force, acts upon them, therefore, injuriously, or beneficially, and they in their turn, poisoned by his baleful influence, when he is depraved, become injurious forces to him by the laws of reaction). — "At once nature itself took on the changed expression; and where all before was gladness and freshness there were now indications of sorrow and decay. Atmospheric influences hitherto unrecognised began to be noted; there was felt a chill in the morning, a dearth of magnetic heat at noon-tide, and a universal deadness at the approach of night, which began to be looked upon with alarm. For a change in the object must accompany every change in the subject. Until this point was reached there was nothing to make man afraid of himself and his surroundings".

"And as he plunged deeper and deeper into matter, he lost his consciousness of the subtler forms of existence, and attributed all the antagonism he experienced to unknown causes. The conflict continued to wax stronger, and, in consequence of his ignorance, man fell a readier victim. There were exceptions among the race then, as there are now, whose finer perceptive faculties outgrew, or kept ahead, of the advancing materialisation; and they alone, in course of events, could feel and recognise the influences of these earliest progeny of the earth."

"Time came when an occasional appearance was viewed with alarm, and was thought to be an omen of evil, Recognising this fear on the part of man, the elementals ultimately came to realise for him the dangers he apprehended, and they banded together to terrify him". — (They reflected back to him his own fears in a concrete form, sufficiently intelligent, perhaps, to take some malicious pleasure in it, for man in propelling into space a force of any kind is met by a reactionary force, which seems to give exactly what his mind foreshadowed. In the negative coldness of fear, he lays himself open to infesting molecules or atoms which paralyse life, and he falls a victim to his own lack of faith, cheerful courage and hope). "They found strong allies in an order of existence which was generated when physical death made its appearance" (*i.e.*, Elementaries, or Shells); " and their combined forces began to manifest themselves at night, for which man had a dread as being the enemy of his protector, the Sun".

"The elementaries galvanized into activity by the elemental beings began to appear to man under as many varieties of shape as his hopes and fears allowed. And as his ignorance of things spiritual became denser, these agencies brought in an influx of error, which accelerated his spiritual degeneration. Thus, it will be seen that man's neglect of his duty to the nature-spirits is the cause which has launched him into a sea of troubles, that has shipwrecked so many generations of his descendants. Famines, plagues, wars, and other catastrophes are not so disconnected with the agency of nature-spirits as it might appear to the sceptical mind".

It is therefore evident that the world of man exercises a controlling power over this invisible world of "elementals". Even in the most remote and inaccessible haunts of nature, where we may imagine halcyon days of an innocent bliss elapsing in poetic peace and beauty for the more harmless of these irresponsible, evanescent offspring of nature's teeming bosom, they must inevitably, sooner or later, yield up their peaceful sovereignty to the greater monarch, man; who usually comes with a harsh and discordant influence, like the burning sirocco of the desert, like the overwhelming avalanche from the silent peaks of snow, or the earthquake, convulsing and tearing to atoms the beauty of gardens, palaces, cities. It is said that elementals "*die*"; it is presumable that at such times they die by myriads, when the whole surface of the earth becomes changed from the unavoidable passing away of nature's wildernesses, the peaceful homes of bird and beast, as the improving, commercial, money-grasping man — that contradiction of God, that industrious destroyer, who lives at war with beauty, peace, and goodness — appears upon the scene. These may be called poetical rhapsodies: yet poetry is, in a mysterious way, closely allied to that hidden truth which has its birth on the soul-plane, and the imagination of man is, according to Eliphas Lévi, a clairvoyant and magical faculty — "the wand of the magician".

To speak of elementals *dying*, is to use a word which expresses for us *change of condition*; the passing from one sphere of life to another, or from one plane of consciousness to another. This to the sensual man is "death". But there is *no* death — it is merely a passing from one phase of existence to another. Hence the elementals lose the forms they once held, changing their plane of consciousness, and appearing in other forms.

We have shown somewhat of the mysterious way in which man acts upon these invisible denizens of his soul-world, and by which he incurs a certain responsibility. By the dynamic power of thought and will it is done — as everything is done. The elementals pushed by man, as by a superior force, off that equilibrium of harmony with pure, innocent nature, which they originally maintained when our planet was young, have been transformed into powers of evil, which man brings upon himself as retribution — the reaction of that force he ignorantly sets in motion when he breaks the beneficent laws of nature. Originally dependant upon him, and capable of aiding him in a thousand ways when he is wise and good, they have become his enemies, who thwart him at every turn, and guard the secrets of their abodes with none the less implacable sternness because they are probably only semi-conscious of the functions they perform. It is nature acting through them — the great Cosmic Consciousness, which forbids that desecrating footsteps shall invade the holy precincts of her stupendous life-secrets. But to the spiritual man — the god — these secrets open of themselves, like a hand laden with gifts, readily unclosing to a favourite and deserving child.

Giving forth a current of evil, and sinking therefrom into a state of bestial ignorance, man has enveloped himself in clouds of darkness which assume monstrous shapes threatening to overwhelm him. A wicked man is generally a coward, because he lives in a state of perpetual dread of the reactionary effect of the evil forces he has set in motion. These are volumes of elemental forms banded together, and swaying like the thunderclouds of a gathering storm.

To disperse these, his own spiritual mind must ray forth the light reflected from the Source of Light — Omniscience. In the astral atmospheres of the spiritual man, there are no clouds, and fear is unknown. In the mental world of the innocent and pure, those are only forms of gracious beauty, as lovely as the shapes of nature's innocent embryons, which reveal themselves in the forests, the running streams, the floating breeze, and in company with the birds and flowers, to the clairvoyant sight of those nature-lovers before whom she withdraws her veils, communing with their souls by an intuitional speech which fills them with rapturous admiration. It is not only the learned scientist who may read Nature's marvellous revelations ; for she whispers them with maternal tenderness into the open ears of babes, where they remain ever safe from desecration, and are cherished as the soul's innocent delights in hours of isolation from the busy, jarring world.

The spiritual soul is ever looking beneath nature's material veils for *correspondences*. Every natural object *means* something else to such penetrating vision — a vision which begins to be spontaneously exercised by the soul when it has fairly reached that stage of spiritual evolution; and to this silent exploration many a secret meaning reveals itself by object-pictures, which awaken reflection and inquiry as to the why and wherefore. Thus the spiritual man drinks, as it were, from nature's own hand the pure waters of an inexhaustible spring — that occult knowledge which feeds his soul, and aids in forming for him a beautiful and powerful astral body. And Nature becomes invested to his penetrating sight with a beauty she never wore before, and which the clay-blinded eyes of animal man can never behold. Such a man would enter the isolated haunts of the purer nature-spirits with gentle footsteps, and loving thoughts. To him the breeze is wafted wooingly, the streams whisper music, and everything wears an aspect of loving joyousness, and inviting confidence. Beside the rigid material forms, he sees their "aromal counterparts": everything is life; the very stones live, and have a consciousness suited to their state: and he feels as if every atom of his own body vibrated into unison with the living things about him — as if *all were one flesh*. To injure a single thing would be impossible to him. Such is the soul-condition of the perfect man, to whom evil has become impossible.

An Adept has written — "Every thought of man upon being evolved passes into another world and becomes an active entity by associating itself — coalescing, we might term it — with an

Elemental — that is to say, with one of the semi-intelligent forces of the kingdoms. It survives as an active intelligence — a creature of the mind's begetting — for a longer or shorter period, proportionate with the original intensity of the cerebral action which, generated it. Thus, a good thought is perpetuated as an active, beneficent power, an evil one as a maleficent demon. And so man is continually peopling his current in space with the offspring of his fancies, desires, impulses, and passions: a current which redacts upon any sensitive or nervous organization which comes in contact with it, in proportion to its dynamic intensity. . . . The Adept evolves these shapes consciously, other men throw them off unconsciously".

Therefore, man must be held responsible not only for his outward actions, but his secret thoughts, by which he puts into existence irresponsible entities of more or less maleficent power, if his thoughts be of an evil nature. These are revelations of a deep and abstruse character; but would they have come at all if man had not reached that stage of evolution when it is necessary he should step up into his spiritual kingdom, and rule as a master over his lower self, and as a beneficent god over every department of unintelligent nature ?.

We note the closing words of the Adept's letter; — "The Adept evolves these shapes consciously, other men throw them off unconsciously" In the Adept's soul-world then — the man who has ascended, by self-conquest primarily, into his spiritual kingdom, and who has graduated through years of probation and study in spiritual or occult science — *i.e.*, the White Magician, the Son of God, the inheritor, by spiritual evolution, of divinity — there would reign peace, happiness, beauty, order, absolute harmony with Nature on the side of good. No discordant note, no deformed astral production to embarrass or obstruct the current of divine magnetism he emanates into space — the delicious, soul-purifying, healing, and uplifting aura which radiates from him as from a centre of beneficence to the lower world of struggling humanity. The semi-intelligent forces of nature, the innocent nature spirits, would, in such a soul-world, find an appropriate and harmonious habitat, clustering in waiting obedience upon the behests of a Master, whose every thought-breath would be as an uplifting life.

To such a state and condition of complete harmony with God and Nature must the truly perfect spiritual man ascend by evolution.

THE DIFFERENCE BETWEEN ELEMENTALS AND ELEMENTARIES

FROM the similarity of the terms used to designate two classes of astral beings who are able to communicate with man, a certain confusion has arisen in the public mind, which it would be as well, perhaps, to aid in, removing.

" Elementals" is a term applied to the nature spirits, the living existences which belong peculiarly to the elements they inhabit; " beings of the *mysteria spetialia*" according to Paracelsus, "soul-forms, which will return into their chaos, and who are not capable of manifesting any higher spiritual activity because they do not possess the necessary kind of constitution in which an activity of a spiritual character can manifest itself." . . . . " Matter is connected with Spirit by an intermediate principle which it receives from this Spirit. This intermediate link between matter and Spirit belongs to all the three kingdoms of nature. In the mineral kingdom it is called Stannar, or Trughat; in the vegetable kingdom, Jaffas; and it forms in connection with the vital force of the vegetable kingdom, the Primum Ens, which possesses the highest medicinal properties. ... In the animal kingdom, this semi-material body is called Evestrum, and in human beings it is called the Sidereal Man. Each living being is connected with the Macrocosmos and Microcosmos by means of this intermediate element or Soul, belonging to the Mysterium Magnum from whence it has been received, and whose form and qualities are determined by the quality and quantity of the spiritual and material elements". . . . From this we may infer that the "Elementals", properly speaking, are the "Soul-forms" of the elements they inhabit — the activities and energies of the World-Soul differentiated into forms, endowed with more or less consciousness, and capacities for "feeling", and hours of enjoyment, or pain. But these, never, or rarely, entering any more deeply into dense matter than enabled so to do by their aerial invisible bodies, do not appear upon our gross physical plane otherwise than as forces, energies, or influences. Their Soul-forms are the intermediate link between matter and spirit, resembling the Soul-forms of animals and men, which also form this intermediate link. The difference being that the souls of animals and men have enveloped themselves in a casing of dense matter for the purposes of existence upon the more external planes of life. Consequently, after the death of the external bodies of men and animals, there remain astral remnants which undergo gradual disintegration in the astral atmospheres. These have been termed "Elementaries" ; *i.e.*, "the astral corpses of the dead; the etherial counterpart of the once living person, which will sooner or later be decomposed into its astral elements, as the physical body is dissolved into the elements to which it belongs. The Elementaries of good people have little cohesion and evaporate soon; those of wicked people may exist a longtime; those of suicides, etc., have a life and consciousness of their own as long as a division of principles has not taken place. These are the most dangerous".

In the introduction to "Isis Unveiled", we find the following definition of Elemental Spirits: —

"The creatures evolved in the four kingdoms of earth, air, fire, and water, and called by the Kabalists gnomes, sylphs, salamanders, and undines. They may be termed the forces of nature, and will either operate effects as the servile agents of general law, or may be employed by the disembodied spirits — whether pure or impure — and by living adepts of magic and sorcery, to produce desired phenomenal results. *Such* beings never become men". (But there are classes of elemental spirits who do become men, as we shall see further on.)

"Under the general designation of fairies and fays, these spirits of the elements appear in the myth, fable, tradition, and poetry of all nations, ancient and modern. Their names are legion — peris, devs, djins, sylvans, satyrs, fawns, elves, dwarfs, trolls, kobolds, brownies, stromkarls, undines, nixies, salamanders, goblins, banshees, kelpies, prixies, moss people, good people, good neighbours, wild women, men of peace, white ladies, and many more. They have been seen, feared, blessed, banned, and invoked in every quarter of the globe and in every age. These elementals are the principal agents of disembodied but never visible spirits at séances, and the producers of all the phenomena except the 'subjective' ". —

"In the Jewish Kabala the nature spirits were known under the general name of *Shedim*, and divided into four classes. The Persians called them *devs*; the Greeks indistinctly designated them as *demons*; the Egyptians knew them as '*afrites*'. The Ancient Mexicans, says Kaiser, believed in numerous spirit-abodes, into one of which the shades of innocent-children were placed until final disposal; into another, situated in the Sun, ascended the valiant souls of heroes; while the hideous spectres of incorrigible sinners were sentenced to wander and despair in subterranean caves, held in the bonds of the earth-atmosphere, unwilling and unable to liberate themselves. They passed their time in communicating with mortals, and frightening those who could see them. Some of the African tribes know them as Yowahoos".—

Of the ideas of Proclus on this subject it is said in "Isis Unveiled" : —

"He held that the four elements are all filled with 'demons', maintaining with Aristotle that the Universe is full, and that there is no void in nature. The demons of earth, air, fire, and water, are of an elastic, ethereal, semi-corporeal essence. It is these classes which officiate as intermediate agents between the gods and men. Although lower in intelligence than the sixth order of the higher demons, these beings preside directly over the elements and organic life. They direct the growth, the inflorescence, the properties, and various changes of plants. They are the personified ideas or virtues shed from the heavenly *ule* into the inorganic matter; and, as the vegetable kingdom is one remove higher than the mineral, these emanations from the celestial gods take form in the plant, and become *its soul*. It is that which Aristotle's doctrine terms the 'form' in the three principles of natural bodies, classified by him as *privation*, matter, and form. His philosophy teaches that besides the original matter, another principle is necessary to complete the triune nature of every particle, and this is 'form'; an invisible, but still, in an ontological sense of the work, a substantial being, really distinct from matter proper. This, in an animal or a plant, besides the bones, the flesh, the nerves, the brains, and the blood, in the former; and besides the pulpy matter, tissues, fibres, and juice in the latter, which blood and juice, by circulating through the veins and fibres, nourishes all parts of both animal and plant; and besides the animal spirits, which are the principles of motion, and the chemical energy which is transformed into vital force in the green leaf, there must be a substantial form, which Aristotle called in the horse, the *horse's soul*; and Proclus, the *demon* of every mineral, plant, or animal, and the mediaeval philosophers, the *elementary spirits* of the four kingdoms".

—

"According to the ancient doctrines, the soulless elemental spirits were evolved by the ceaseless motion inherent in the astral light. Light is force, and the latter is produced by *will*. As this will proceeds from an intelligence which cannot err, for it has nothing of the material organs of human thought in it, being the superfine pure emanation of the highest divinity itself — (Plato's 'Father') — it proceeds from the beginning of time, according to immutable laws, to evolve the elementary fabric requisite for subsequent generations of what we term human races. All of the latter, whether belonging to this planet or to some other of the myriads in space, have their earthly bodies evolved in the matrix out of the bodies of a certain class of these elemental beings which have passed away in the invisible worlds". —

Speaking of Pythagoras, Iamblichus, and other Greek philosophers, "Isis" says: —

"The universal ether was not, in their eyes, simply a something stretching, tenantless, throughout the expanse of heaven; it was a boundless ocean peopled, like our familiar seas, with monstrous and minor creatures, and having in its every molecule the germs of life. Like the finny tribes which swarm in our oceans and smaller bodies of water, each kind having its 'habitat' in some spot to which it is curiously adapted; some friendly and some inimical to man; some pleasant and some frightful to behold; some seeking the refuge of quiet nooks and land-locked harbours, and some traversing great areas of water, the various races of the elemental spirits were believed by them to inhabit the different portions of the great ethereal ocean, and to be exactly adapted to their respective conditions "

"Lowest in the scale of being are those invisible creatures called by the Kabalists the 'elementary'. There are three distinct classes of these. The highest, in intelligence and cunning, are the so-called terrestrial spirits, the 'larvae', or shadows of those who have lived on earth, have refused all spiritual light, remained and died deeply immersed in the mire of matter, and from whose sinful souls the immortal spirit has gradually separated. The second class is composed of invisible antitypes of men 'to be' born. No form can come into objective existence — from the highest to the lowest — before the abstract idea of this form, or as Aristotle would call it, the privation of this form — is called forth. . . . These models, as yet devoid of immortal spirits, are 'Elementals' properly speaking, 'psychic embryos' — which, when their time arrives, die out of the invisible world, and are born into this visible one as human infants, receiving *in transitu* that divine breath called spirit, which completes the perfect man. This class cannot communicate objectively with man.

"The third class of Elementals proper, which never evolve into human beings, but occupy, as it were, a specific step of the ladder of being, and, by comparison with the others, may properly be called nature-spirits, or cosmic agents of nature, each being confined to its own element, and never transgressing the bounds of others. These are what Tertullian called 'the princes of the powers of the air'.

"This class is believed to possess but one of the three attributes of man. They have neither immortal souls nor tangible bodies; only astral forms, which partake, in a distinguishing degree, of the element to which they belong, and also of the Ether. They are a combination of sublimated matter and a rudimental mind. Some are changeless, but still have no separate individuality, acting collectively so to say. Others, of certain elements and species, change form under a fixed law which Kabalists explain. The most solid of their bodies is ordinarily just immaterial enough to escape perception by our physical eyesight, but not so unsubstantial but that they can be perfectly recognised by the inner or clairvoyant vision. They not only exist, and can all live in ether, but can handle and direct it for the production of physical effects, as readily as we can compress air or water for the same purpose by pneumatic or hydraulic apparatus; in which occupation they are readily helped by the 'human elementary'. More than this; they can so condense it as to make to themselves tangible bodies, which by their Protean powers they can cause to assume such likenesses as they choose, by taking as their models the portraits they find stamped in the memory of the persons present. It is not necessary that the sitter should be thinking at the moment of the one represented. His image may have faded away years before. The mind receives indelible impression even from chance acquaintance, or persons encountered but once".

"If Spiritualists are anxious to keep strictly dogmatic in their notions of the Spirit-World, they must not set *scientists* to investigate their phenomena in the true experimental spirit. The attempt would most surely result in a partial re-discovery of the magic of old — that of Moses and Paracelsus. Under the deceptive beauty of some of their apparitions, they might find some day the sylphs and fair undines of the Rosicrucians playing in the currents of *psychic* and *odic* force".

"Already Mr. Crookes, who fully credits the *being*, feels that under the fair skin of Katie, covering a simulacrum of heart borrowed partially from the medium and the circle, there is NO SOUL !. And the learned authors of the "Unseen Universe", abandoning their "electro-biological" theory, begin to perceive in the universal ether the *possibility* that it is a photographic album of *En-Soph* the Boundless".

" We are far from believing that all the spirits that communicate at circles are of the classes called 'Elemental' and 'Elementary' . " Many, especially among those who control the medium subjectively to speak, write, and otherwise act in various ways, are human, disembodied spirits. Whether the majority of such spirits are good or *bad*, largely depends on the private morality of the medium, much on the circle present, and a great deal on the intensity and object of their purpose. . . . But in any case, human spirits can *never* materialize themselves in *propria persona*, &c. [By which it is, doubtless, meant that the *full* individually is not present: the higher principles, the *true spirit*, having ascended to its appropriate house, from which there is no attraction to earth. That which materialises would be an elemental, or elementals moulding their fluidic forms in the likeness of the departed human being; or, on the other hand, considering and revivifying, the atomic remnants of the sidereal encasement, or astral body, still left undissipated in the soul-world].

In "Art Magic" we find the following pertinent remarks: "There are some features of mediumship, especially amongst those persons known as 'physical force mediums', which long since should have awakened the attention of philosophical spiritualists to the fact that there were influences kindred only with animal natures at work somewhere, and unless the agency of certain classes of Elemental Spirits was admitted into the category of occasional control, humanity has at times assumed darker shades than we should be willing to assign to it. Unfortunately in discussing these subjects, there are many barriers to the attainment of truth on this subject. Courtesy and compassion alike protest against pointing to illustrations in our own time, whilst prejudice and ignorance intervene to stifle inquiry respecting phenomena, which a long lapse of time has left us free to investigate".

"The judges whose ignorance and superstition disgraced the Witchcraft trials of the sixteenth and seventeenth centuries, found a solvent for all occult, or even suspicious circumstances, in the control of 'Satan and his imps'. The modern Spiritualists, with few exceptions, are equally stubborn in attributing everything that transpires in Spiritualistic circles, even to the wilful *cunningly contrived preparations for deception* on the part of pretended media, to the influence of disembodied human spirits — good, bad, or indifferent; but the author's own experience, confirmed by the assurances of wise-teaching spirits, impels him to assert that the tendencies to exhibit animal proclivities, whether mental, passional, or phenomenal, are most generally produced by Elementals."

"The rapport with this realm of beings is generally due to certain proclivities in the individual; or, when whole communities are affected, the cause proceeds from revolutionary movements in the realms of astral fluid; these continually affect the Elementals, who, in combination with low undeveloped spirits of humanity

(Elementaries), avail themselves of magnetic epidemics to obsess susceptible individuals, and sympathetically affect communities."

In the introduction to "Isis Unveiled", we find the following definition of Elementary Spirits: —

"Properly, the disembodied *souls* of the depraved: these souls, having at some time prior to death, separated from themselves their divine spirits, and so lost their chance of immortality. Eliphas Levi and some other Kabalists make little distinction between Elementary Spirits, who have been men, and those beings which people the elements and are the blind forces of nature. Once divorced from their bodies, these souls (also called "astral bodies") of purely materialistic persons, are irresistibly attracted to the earth, where they live a temporary and finite life amid elements congenial to their gross natures. From having never, during their, natural lives, cultivated this spirituality, but subordinated it to the material and gross, they are now unfitted for the lofty career of the pure, disembodied being, for whom the atmosphere of earth is stifling and mephitic, and whose attractions are all away from it. After a more or less prolonged period of time these material souls will begin to disintegrate, and finally, like a column of mist, be dissolved, atom by atom, in the surrounding elements." —

"After the death of the depraved and the wicked, arrives the critical moment. If during life the ultimate and desperate effort of the inner-self to reunite itself with the faintly-glimmering ray of its divine parent is neglected; if this ray is allowed to be more and more shut out by the thickening crust of matter, the soul, once freed from the body, follows its earthly attractions, and is magnetically drawn into and held within the dense fogs of the material atmosphere. Then it begins to sink lower and lower, until it finds itself, when returned to consciousness, in what the ancients termed Hades. The annihilation of such a soul is never instantaneous; it may last centuries perhaps; for nature never proceeds by jumps and starts, and the astral soul, being formed of elements, the law of evolution must bide its time. Then begins the fearful law of compensation, the *Yin-Youan* of the Buddhists. This class of spirits are called the Terrestrial, or *earthly* elementary, in contradistinction to the other classes." (They frequent séance rooms, &c.) —

Of the danger of meddling in occult matters before understanding the elementals and elementaries, " Isis" says, in the case of a rash intruder :—

"The spirit of harmony and union will depart from the elements, disturbed by the imprudent hand; and the currents of blind forces will become immediately infested by numberless creatures of matter and instinct — the bad daemons of the theurgists, the devils of theology; the gnomes, salamanders, sylphs, and undines will assail the rash performer under multifarious aerial forms. Unable to invent anything, they will search your memory to its very depths; hence the nervous exhaustion and mental oppression of certain sensitive natures at spiritual circles. The Elementals will bring to light long-forgotten remembrances of the past; forms, images, sweet mementos, and familiar sentences, long since faded from our own remembrance, but vividly preserved in the inscrutable depths of our memory and on the astral tablets of the imperishable ' BOOK OF LIFE' ". —

Paracelsus speaks of *Xeni Nephidei*: " Elemental spirits that give men occult powers over visible matter, and then feed on their brains, often causing thereby insanity".

"Man rules potentially over all lower existences than himself", says the author of "Art Magic", but woe to him, who by seeking aid, counsel, or assistance, from lower grades of being, binds himself to them; henceforth he may rest assured they will become his parasites and associates, and as their instincts — like those of the animal kingdom — are strong in the particular direction of their nature, they are powerful to disturb, annoy, prompt to evil, and avail themselves of the contact induced by man's invitation to drag him down to their own level. The legendary idea of evil compacts between man and the 'Adversary' is not wholly mythical. Every wrong-doer signs that compact with spirits who have sympathy 'with his evil actions'.

"Except for the purposes of scientific investigation, or with a view of strengthening ourselves against the silent and mysterious promptings to evil that beset us on every side, we warn mere curiosity-seekers, or persons ambitious to attach the legions of an unknown world to their service, against any attempts to seek communion with Elemental spirits, or beings of any grade lower than man. *Beings below mortality can grant nothing that mortality ought to ask*. They can only serve man in some embryonic department of nature, and man must stoop to their state before they can thus reach him." ..." Knowledge is only good for us when we can apply it judiciously. Those who investigate for the sake of science, or with a view of enlarging the narrow boundaries of man's egotistical opinions, may venture much further into the realms of the unknown than curiosity-seekers, or persons who desire to apply the secrets of being to selfish purposes. It may be as well also for man to remember that he and his planet are not *the all* of being, and that, besides the revelations included in the stupendous outpouring called 'Modern Spiritualism', there are many problems yet to be solved in human life and planetary existences, which spiritualism does not cover, nor ignorance and prejudice dream of." . . . "Besides these considerations, we would warn man of the many subtle, though invisible, enemies which surround him, and, rather by the instinct of their embryotic natures than through *malice prepense*, seek to lay siege to the garrison of the human heart. We would advise him, moreover, that into that sacred entrenchment no power can enter, save by invitation of the soul itself. Angels may solicit, or demons may tempt, but none can compel the spirit within to action, unless it first surrenders the *will* to the investing power." —

From the "Theosophist" of July 1886, we make the following extract, bearing upon the subject of the loss of immortality by soul-death, and the dangers of Black Magic, " It is necessary to say a few words as regards the real nature of soul-death, and the ultimate fate of a black magician. The soul, as we have explained above, is an isolated drop in the ocean of cosmic life. This current of cosmic life is but the light and the aura of the Logos. Besides the Logos, there are innumerable other existences, both spiritual and astral, partaking of this life and living in it. These beings have special affinities with particular emotions of the human soul, and particular characteristics of the human mind. They have, of course, a definite individual existence of their own, which lasts up to the end of the Manwantara. There are three ways in which a soul may cease to retain its special individuality. Separated from its Logos, which is, as it were, its source, it may not acquire a strong and abiding individuality of its own, and may in course of time be reabsorbed into the current of universal life. This is real soul-death. It may also place itself *en rapport* with a spiritual or elemental existence by evoking it, and concentrating its attention and regard upon it for purposes of black magic and Tantric worship. In such a case it transfers its individuality to such existence and is sucked up into it, as it were. In such a case the black magician lives in such a being, and as such a being he continues until the end of Manwantara."

A good deal of highly interesting information on the subject of Elementals and Elementaries is to be found in the numbers of THE PATH for May, June, and July, of this year. A few of the points contained in these articles maybe mentioned here, but the reader is strongly recommended to study these articles, entitled

"Conversations on Occultism", for himself. According to the writer:—

An Elemental is a centre of force, without intelligence, as we understand the word, without moral character or tendencies similar to ours, but capable of being directed in its movements by human thoughts, which may, consciously or not, give it any form, and endow it to a certain extent with what we call intelligence. We give them form by a species of thought which the mind does not register — involuntary and unconscious thought — "as one person might shape an Elemental so as to seem like an insect, and not be able to tell whether he had thought of such a thing or not". The Elemental world interpenetrates this one and Elementals are constantly being attracted to, or repelled from, human beings, taking the prevailing colour of their thoughts. Time and space, as we understand them, do not exist for Elementals. They can be seen clairvoyantly in the shapes they assume under different influences, and they do many of the phenomena of the *séance* room. Light and the concentrated attention of anyone make a disturbance in the magnetism of a room, interfering with their work in that respect. At *séances* Elementaries also are present; these are "shells," or half-dead human beings. The Elementaries are not all bad, however, but the worst are the strongest, because the most attracted to material life. They are all helped and galvanized into action by Elementals.

Contact with these beings has a deteriorating effect in all cases. Clairvoyants see in the astral light surrounding a person the images of people or events that have made an impression on that person's mind, and they frequently mistake these echoes and reflections for astral realities; only the trained seer can distinguish. The whole astral world is full of illusions.

Elementals have not got *being* such as mortals have. There are different classes for the different planes of nature. Each class is confined to its own plane, and many can never be recognised by men. The Elemental world is a strong factor in Karma. Formerly, when men were less selfish and more spiritual, the elementals were friendly. They have become unfriendly by reason of man's indifference to, and want of sympathy with, the rest of creation. Man has also coloured the astral world with his own selfish and brutal thoughts, and produced an atmosphere of evil which he himself breathes, When men shall cultivate feelings of brotherly affection for each other, and of sympathy with Nature, the Elementals will change their present hostile attitude for one of helpfulness.

Elementals aid in the performance of phenomena produced by adepts. They also enter the sphere of unprotected persons, and especially of those who study occultism, thus precipitating the results of past Karma.

The adepts are reluctant to speak of elementals for two reasons. Because it is useless, as people could not understand the subject in their present state of intellectual and spiritual development; and because, if any knowledge of them were given, some persons might be able to come into contact with them to their own detriment and that of the world. In the present state of universal selfishness and self-seeking, the elementals would be employed to work evil, as they are in themselves colourless, taking their character from those who employ them. The adepts, therefore, keep back or hide the knowledge of these beings from men of science, and from the world in general. By and bye, however, material science will rediscover black magic, and then will come a war between the good and evil powers, and the evil powers will be overcome, as always happens in such cases. Eventually all about the Elementals will be known to men — when they have developed intellectually, morally, and spiritually sufficiently to have that knowledge without danger.

Elementals guard hidden treasures; they obey the adepts, however, who could command the use of untold wealth if they cared to draw upon these hidden deposits

www.ingramcontent.com/pod-product-compliance
Lightning Source LLC
LaVergne TN
LVHW041502070426
835507LV00009B/762